Anna Brenken

Dresden

Ellert & Richter
Verlag
Die weiße Reihe

Anna Brenken, born 1939 in Essen, lives in Hamburg and works as a freelance journalist for several newspapers, magazines and journals. She is specialized in art, literature and theatre. Publications in the Ellert & Richter Verlag: Künstlerdorf Worpswede, Hamburg – Spaziergänge.

Literature:
Michael W. Alpatow: Die Dresdner Galerie Alte Meister, Dresden 1966
Barock in Dresden. Hrsg. von Ulli Arnold und Werner Schmidt, Leipzig 1986
Dresden zur Goethezeit 1760–1815.
Hrsg. von Günter Jäckel, Hanau 1988
Wolfgang Hänsch: Die Semperoper, Berlin 1986
Volker Helas: Architektur in Dresden 1800–1900, Braunschweig 1985
Fritz Löffler: Das alte Dresden, Leipzig 1989
Wolfgang Paul: . . . zum Beispiel Dresden.
Schicksal einer Stadt, Frankfurt/M. 1964

Illustration credits:
Gert von Bassewitz/Transglobe Agency, Hamburg, S.: 14/15
Eberhard Grames/Bilderberg, Hamburg, S.: 32/33, Titel
Jürgens Ost + Europa Photo, Köln, S.: 6, 12, 18/19, 21, 22/23, 24, 25, 26/27, 28/29, 29 o., 30/31, 34/35, 36/37, 37 u., 38/39, 40, 41, 43, 48/49, 50/51
Urs F. Kluyver, Hamburg, S.: 27 u., 29 u., 37 o., 44/45
Gert Koshofer, Bergisch Gladbach, S.: 27 o.
Rudi Meisel/Visum, Hamburg, S.: 42/43, 46/47
Rolf Nobel/Visum, Hamburg, S.: 10/11
Archiv Richter, Hamburg, S.: 5, 8, 9, 13

Text and captions: Anna Brenken, Hamburg
Translation: David Brayshaw, Hamburg
Design: Hartmut Brückner, Bremen
Setting: Fotosatz Wahlers, Langwedel
Lithography: Rüdiger + Doepner, Bremen
Print: C. H. Wäser, Bad Segeberg
Binding: Buchbinderei Klemme, Bielefeld

Contents

His heart shall always rest in Dresden. It was the wish of a mighty ruler. His last wish in a fulfilled life, in which he achieved more than most of us are granted. Thus the resting place of the heart of Friedrich August I., called August der Starke, hereditary elector of Saxony, King of Poland, born in Dresden 1670 and died in Warsaw 1733, is in the Hofkirche of Dresden, built by his pious son and successor Friedrich August II. (1696–1763).

The centre of Dresden was constructed under the aegis of these two princes of the Saxon House of Wettin, the residential city of the Baroque on the Elbe, which today attracts people from all corners of the world to Saxony.

No other town was damaged in the War as much as Dresden. After experiencing the fire storm of the Allied bombing raid of the night of the 13 to 14 February 1945, Gerhart Hauptmann wrote at the age of 82, "those who had forgotten how to cry, learnt it again in the destruction of Dresden". The rebuilding of the city today seems a wonder to those who had survived the inferno at that time. The Zwinger was first to be restored – built by the architect Daniel Pöppelmann, between 1710 and 1732, for the Saxon Sonnenkönig as a princely court for festivals and pageants of truly accomplished elegance. The Hofkirche, the Semper Opera House are reconstructed. The Schloss, one of the most imposing pieces in the jigsaw of the town skyline of Dresden follows as the last major act of restauration.

The existence of beautiful Dresden – today not without scars: the visible destruction of war and Socialist development and the inner trauma of a jaunted Socialism – derives from two pieces of good fortune. The geographic location where the town and the surrounding hilly riverscape fit together in perfect harmony. The influence of important personalities of the Arts and Sciences, who were attracted by the brilliant town of culture at the base of the hills of the Elbe, where the vines grow and where it is quite splendid to reside and live, if you only let people do so.

Not only the Baroque age raised the Saxon provincial town to the heights of a secret worldly centre of culture, of spirit. Dresden celebrates many achievements as we will see in the following chapters. Architects, artists, Renaissance craftsmen, the Rococo, Classicism, the Gründerzeit and the Jugendstil all left their mark. The German Klassik, the age of romantic literature and creative art, had its main sphere here with a strong field of influence. Music was also dominant here in the Elb-Florence in the 19th century. The German composers Carl Maria von Weber and Richard Wagner succeeded against the Italians. Gottfried Semper erected one of the most splendid opera houses of Europe on the Elbe. Soon lavish villas of the Gründerzeit and Jugendstil rowed themselves along the Weißer Hirsch, the chain of moraine hills on the north bank of the Elbe. One was wealthy in Dresden at the turn of the century and one showed it.

Painters of the "Brücke" established the Expressionist revolution in Dresden in 1905. The twentieth century passed in this city with alternating powerful changes between periods of flourishment and periods of destruction. The "beauty of the Elbe" has, retained one thing, which was characteristic of the whole centuries of its existence: Dresden was never the seat of a powerful political force, but was often – as we will see – worldwide influential in the Arts. Such a city is a place of yearning. To Dresden, to Dresden ...

The Elbe is patient. Its water is murky black at Dresden. A lot happens to its flow along the 1144 kilometre path between the spring in the Riesengebirge and the estuary at Cuxhaven. Here it is able to dissipate into the North Sea along a breadth of 15 kilometres. The gentle meanders, which lose their name Labe at the Czechoslovakian border, are only 120 metres wide at Dresden. Fortunately! Otherwise there would probably not have been a town at all. It was an easy crossing place for travellers on the ancient trading route between west and east. There was even a stone built bridge at the end the 13th century across the Elbe. A document of 1216 mentions, "… in civitate nostra Dreseden." Dresden acquired town rights, and was considerably developed from the original Slavic village of Drez-dany.

The flourishment of a town in the Middle Ages is best documented in its churches. Three churches go back to this period in Dresden, which help to form the urban cha-racter in differing ways. The Frauenkirche from the 11th century is the oldest. It was probably founded as a missionary base from the monastery of Hersfeld. It has been Dresden's most important and largest church throughout the centuries. In 1772 the city counsellors appointed the architect Georg Bähr to build a new building fitting to the needs of the large Protestant community and the Zeitgeist, the spirit of Baroque monumentality. Bähr crowned this new house of God, having a capacity for 4000 people, with a sandstone dome. The mighty stone bell over the roofs of the city became thy symbol of Dresden. Only the dome of St Peters in Rome and the church of Santa Maria della Salute in Venice were more famous. If you stand in front of the Frauenkirche today, you are stricken by sadness. This mighty building collapsed in on itself on 15th February 1945, after the fire storm. The ruin is a dramatic monument against war.

The foundation of the Kreuzkirche goes back into the 13th century. Over its 800 years history it has been destroyed four times by fire and once when the tower collapsed. After its reconstruction in 1955 it has again housed the world famous Kreuzchor of Dresden. Many who attended the Kreuzschule belonging to the church, have later made their careers as singers. The tenor Peter Schreier and the bass baritone Theo Adam are examples.

The Baroque tower of the former Gothic Dreikönigskirche dominates the Neustadt on the right bank of the Elbe. It was also often destroyed. August der Starke even moved it stone for stone and rebuilt it on another site in 1732. The church was in the way of his plans for building the Neustadt where he created a boulevard, the present Straße der Befreiung. If you walk through Dresden, you often look up. A variety of towers dominate the skyline. It is a pleasure

Bernardo Bellotto, known as Canaletto (1720−1780), was unique in capturing Dresden during the Baroque period. This picture shows the Frauenkirche as seen from the Neumarkt.

for those who know to stand on the Augustusbrücke, which forms the bow between the Altstadt and the Neustadt and identify the towers in a row. The first to build out into the sky was Moritz Count of Saxony (1521–1553). This typical Renaissance Prince transformed the small provincial Saxon town into a European cultural metropolis.

Moritz involved himself in international politics. He was awarded the Kurwürde, the electoral right to choose the Kaiser, in 1547. At 32 years he died very young. But he gave his seat such a glory as no other Wettiner before him and it was reached again by another only 150 years later: August der Starke. Moritz was a creative artist prince. He needed money to fulfil his plans. A lot of money. This flowed mainly from Annaberg and Friedberg in the Erzgebirge. 30 percent of the European silver production came from the mines of the town of Annaberg in the 16th century. The vaults of the Prince were also filled by the proceeds from iron mines of Freiberg. Moritz founded the Fürstenschulen in Pforta, Meißen and Grimma. Most of all, he brought artists from all parts of Europe to Dresden. Titian painted him and his fellow countrymen built for him. His castle, a four winged formal Renaissance building complex became a total art composition between architecture, sculpture and painting. The Stallhof, restored today, was famous in the whole of Europe as the location for mighty duelling tournaments between knights and fighting contests. He erected an arsenal – today the site of the Albertinum.

His hunting castle is today one of Dresdens most popular places to visit. If you cross the bridge lined with heroic stone figures – the castle is situated in the middle of a lake full of carp – you can not only saturate yourself in the old magnificence but also drink coffee there.

The splendid residence of Moritz has fallen to the passage of time over the centuries, to the renewal desires of his successors, and finally the victim of the bombing. A stone carving of Adam and Eve can be found on the Georgentor still standing, showing their grief at the loss of paradise. Moritz himself can be found not far away from the Georgentor on the Brühlsche Terrasse, which the Renaissance prince created in the 16th century as a promenade for his beautiful residence. The stone monument, the very first monument in Dresden depicts the prince presenting the sword of honour to his brother August. The first period of flourishment of Dresden was at an end. The town was fortunate in another way during the following century. It was mostly spared from the effects of the Thirty Years War.

The Brühlsche Garten has always been a place for sauntering. The background has the tower of the castle and of the Hofkirche.

His intellect and his politeness were as large as the beauty of his appearance. He was terribly attractive to women. This was the observation of a contemporary nobleman of the effect of August der Starke. The name of the era of this despotic ruler of the Elbe is the "Augusteische Zeitalter". There was a good reason. This visionary of the Saxon throne created one of the most beautiful residences of Europe: the Elb-Florence. In his dreams he planned a Venice on the Elbe. The river bows being a Grand Canal. The cultural landscape between Pirna and Meissen crossed by artificial waterways, sweetly fringed by numerous palaces. This Grand Idea remained unfulfilled.

However August's uncompleted work was magnificent enough. When the serious and completely unworldly reared Prussian prince Friedrich, who later became known as the "Great", visited the Small-Venice in 1732 at the age of twenty, his eyes must have almost popped out of his head. Coming from a raw Potsdam, he saw a royal residence in which everything was centred on beauty. The main aim was to transform life into one long celebration. A royal town with a glittering Schloss and twenty palaces. The Saxon aristocracy competed with their ruler in creating the most charming domicile.

The creative Friedrich August I., as he was called as Saxon elector, was educated at an early life to be a child of this world. He could speak French, Italian, Spanish. He travelled to Copenhagen at the age of 14 to visit his uncle, the King of Denmark, who fostered culture. He saw the art collections of Paris and Madrid. His most influential visual scenario was Italy. He loved Venice. This love was shared by his teacher of architecture, the architect Caspar von Klengel, under whose influence the bye-law was passed that nothing should be built which would "be against the charms of the town or badly effect a neighbour".

August was an ambitious aesthetic and patron of the arts. In 1694 at the age of 24 he was made Elector of Saxony. Three years later he managed the jump onto the Throne of Poland, after he was converted into a Catholic. Poland was a highly cultivated Empire at that time. This crowning was a welcome expansion of his power to the art loving August.

However he mainly built in Dresden. He assembled artisan craftsmen from all over Europe. If they were good, they were extremely well rewarded. Matthäus Daniel Pöppelmann came from Herford at the age of 18. Inspired by the international flair of the Saxon Court, he was to become August's most famous architect. The sculptor Balthasar Permoser from Traunstein came to Dresden first in 1689. This gifted craftsman trio was complimented by Johann Melchior Dinglinger from Biberach an der Riß. This goldsmith was a genius and his prince saw it too. Both were happy. Dinglinger created the most beautiful and delicate jewelry of the Baroque. His works of art sparkle and glitter with precious stones. Today they are an unravelled treat for the eye. This precious collection can be admired in the Grünes Gewölbe. Among it is the wonder of the world in jewelry, the depiction of a Hofstaat, a princely court of an Indian Great Mogul made of gold, silver, diamonds, jasper, rubies, sapphires, emeralds and red coral. The master worked seven years on this piece together with his 14 assistants. Dinglinger studied all the Indian literature of the time to do it. His Hofstaat in miniature became a forerunner in the style of the age. August der Starke had to dig deep into his pocket to pay for this magnificent work of art.

The size of Dinglinger's respectability can be judged by the fact that the Tsar of Russia was used to staying with him when he came to Dresden. When the Court Jeweller died in 1731 he was given a magnificent burial. His coffin was escorted by 14 white horses. Dinglinger and the Italian trained sculptor Permoser often worked together. The clever result of another teamwork was the Zwinger. Pöppelmann created the architecture and Permoser the statues. The architect was 60 and the sculptor 50 years old, when they started the most major project of their lives work. Their royal client had something quite magnificent in mind. The Zwinger was to be a part of a palace complex which stretched down to the Elbe. This was not completed. The Zwinger remained uncompleted and was only finalised by the rather heavy looking building of the Gemäldegalerie, the picture gallery by Gottfried Semper.

The Zwinger with its Kronentor, Pavilion and galleries is in mature Baroque passion. The only thing which is wrong is its name. This describes a previous complex which housed wild animals. The Royal Orangery was a place which the Court could finally use for their excessive festive occasions.

Nothing was too expensive for the King to adorn his rooms. "White Gold" was particularly precious at that time: porcelain. Poor Johann Friedrich Böttger (1682–1719), locked away in the cellars of the Brühlsche Terrasse, experimented so long until he discovered the red Böttger-Stein-

This is the way Canaletto saw the Zwinger complex, which was completed into a square later by the Sempergalerie in the 19th century.

zeug and then white porcelain, the Dresden China. August collected the fragile luxuries, which were soon turned out in piles in nearby Meissen, like a royal squirrel. He even swapped 600 Saxon dragoons for 150 Chinese vases with the Prussian "Soldatenkönig", the father of Friedrich II. The "Dragonervasen" can be seen in the present Porcelain Museum of the Zwinger. August der Starke collected everything that was beautiful. His girlfriends are still talked about in Dresden today. At that time they were respectable "mistresses" at court. Their children – August adopted eight illegitimate children – were adorned with titles and wealth. The Countess Anna Constanze Cosel, who was later extradited, owned Schloss Pillnitz for a time, before its Baroque reconstruction, and the Taschenbergpalais. Both monumental buildings were designed by August's favourite architect Pöppelmann. The Westphalian unceasingly left his trace of beauty, which one can clearly see wondering through Dresden and its surroundings. The Japanese Palace, the reconstruction of the Moritzburg and the Dreikönigskirche, the Friedrichschlößchen in Großsedlitz, the Augustusbrücke. His Grünes Gewölbe in the Schloss is being restored. The building of the Grünes Gewölbe was a democratic act of the despotic Prince August. He opened this treasure and chambers of wonder to the public and thus created one of the first museums of Europe. There was an opera house with seating for 2 000 for the entertainment of his subjects. It was a generous offer for a population of only 35,000. Those who lived in Dresden were urbane and worldly.

The son of August der Starke succeeded in continuing in his own way this peak of art and culture. He was the only child of the King and his wife Christiane Eberhardine, who was known as the "Saxon Betsäule" through her piety. Friedrich August II.

(1696–1763) was mainly educated, like his father, in Italy. He married the daughter of the emperor Maria Josepha from Vienna in 1719.

From his Italian travels, Friedrich August developed a great love for the painting of the country. The Art Collection of Dresden was founded before his time. He was responsible for its character through the Gallery of Old Masters which made into one of the most valuable art collections in the whole world. When the "Sixtinian Madonna" from Raffael arrived, Friedrich August is said to have pushed aside his throne in admiration to hang it in a better light. This picture which he acquired had the importance for the Zwinger as Leonardo da Vinci's "Mona Lisa" for the Louvre. When the archaeologist Winckelmann saw the picture in Dresden in the middle of the 18th century, he praised it by saying; "the Madonna has the face of innocence and at the same time has a rather over-female size, in a satisfying, peaceful posture ..."

Friedrich August brought the Italian painter Bernardo Bellotto, called Canaletto, to the Elbe. His life-like Rococo reflections of the Saxon metropolis are special treasures of the Zwinger. They have marvellous aesthetic quality. They also give precise information on the appearance of Dresden around the middle of the 18th century. Canalettos drawings and paintings, produced during the twenty years he stayed in Dresden were used by restorers after 1945, two hundred years later as a reference. The reconstruction of Baroque Dresden could and still can be possible through the sketches and guidelines of the Italian master.

Another Italian, the architect Gaetano Chiaveri designed the Hofkirche for Friedrich August in 1738. Today you can hear the organ again, which the most famous organ builder Johann Gottfried Silbermann created in the Augustinian Age.

Every blossom whelks. Every golden age fades out in the end. The Augustinian Age ended with the Seven Years War (1756–1763). The child soldier from Prussia, Friedrich II. sieged the art city of the worldling August der Starke and reduced part of this marvellous Baroque on the Elbe into rubble and ashes. The Zwinger was made into a timber store.

The famous view by Canaletto: The artist stood on the right bank of the Elbe looking at the Augustusbrücke with the towers of the Frauen- and Hofkirche situated in the background.

Sunset across the Elbe. The beautiful Baroque elevation of Dresden on the southern bow of the river is already in shadow.

The boats of the Weiße Flotte have moored at the Brühlsche Terrasse.

"... and Dresden will be the Athens for the artist." This was the view of the archaeologist and art historian Johann Joachim Winckelmann who lived in Dresden in the middle of the 18th century. He was the theoretican of classicism, the relearning of the culture of classical Greece.

The country of the Greeks sought after by the soul. Yes, even Goethe came to Dresden. Only Royalty in the castle displayed no interest. The fall of power after the Seven Year War gave rise to a cultural development at provincial level. The Court of Culture was finished. Dresden itself became a town of culture. Mostly painters and writers came. Attracted by the wealth of art, enthused by the beauty of the landscape, in which this Baroque pearl was bedded. A new social culture was created. One of the most beneficial hosts was the Oberkonsistorialrat Christian Gottfried Körner, the father of the poet and freedom fighter Theodor Körner. His guest book in the Neustadt is worth seeing: Goethe, Wieland, Mozart, Herder, the Humboldt brothers and Schlegel, Novalis, Heinrich von Kleist. All debated, played music or held recitals in the Körnerschen Salon.

Friedrich von Schiller was a guest at his friend Körner for two years, during which time he wrote "Don Carlos". His most favourite place was in the summer house of his guest family in the vineyards at Loschwitz on the Elbe. Sometimes he strolled over to the inn at Blasewitz and was served by the inn-keepers daughter Gustel. As you can read he did not forget that young lady. In "Wallensteins Lager", is the following: "What? thunder. That is Gustel from Blasewitz."

Court considered Mozart's operas to be too light-hearted. However the composer came to Dresden in 1790. He fell partially in love with a young beauty and played mostly piano. The "bourgeois Salon", in the Elbe-

stadt was as the peak of the age. The French Revolution was somehow slightly missed. This outraged the poet Jean Paul after a visit.

Heinrich von Kleist came to Dresden for six years in 1803. He lived good and bad as a freelance journalist from the proceeds of the paper he founded, which he named after the antique sun god "Phöbus". He wrote the "Zerbrochenen Krug" and the "Käthchen von Heilbronn". It was probably the happiest time of his life in Dresden.

The biggest attraction for a culturally motivated life around 1800 was the Gemäldegalerie. It was the regular meeting place in the summer of 1789 for their "Galeriegespräche" of the Schlegel brothers, Caroline Schlegel, Novalis, Schelling, Rahel Levin. Goethe enthusiastically described this art collection. The Geheimrat, the privy counsellor from Weimar was a welcome guest in Salons on the Elbe. It was a long told story in the house of the painter Gerhard von Kügelgen to point out at exactly which window Goethe had stood to watch the triumphant march of the Tsar of Russia after the defeat of Napoleon. A small plaque commemorates this today. The flat of the Kügelgens on the second floor of the old house on the Straße der Befreiung in the Neustadt is a museum of Early Romanticism in Dresden since 1981.

These painters of Romanticism are also

This shows how busy the Augustusbrücke was in 1845. One walked between the Neustadt in the north and the Altstadt in the south, with the view topped by the towers of the Hofkirche.

remembered here, who spent important years in the Elbestadt: Caspar David Friedrich and Philipp Otto Runge. Friedrich, born in Greifswald came in 1798. He remained until his death in 1840. From our present day point of view, his allegorical landscape paintings made him one of the most important painters of his period. Some of his major works are carefully stored in the Zwinger: including "Kreuz im Gebirge" and "Zwei Männer in Betrachtung des Mondes". He met Philipp Otto Runge in the Kunstakademie and in the house of Kügelgen in 1801. This young painter had studied at the Copenhagen Academy. He found his style in Dresden. He painted "Die Vier Tageszeiten". Clemens Brentano later described his new powerfully symbolic painting in a letter to the painter as the lonely path "to reconstruct lost paradise from its necessity".

An important influence on Runge apart from Friedrich was the Dresden poet and translator Ludwig Tieck. He worked as a dramatist at the Hoftheater and was the centre point of literary life. The recital evenings at Hofrat Tieck at the Altmarkt were famous. His name was vital to the history of the German acceptance of Shakespeare. The Schlegel/Tieck translation of the Shakespeare plays is still valid. Today we also know that the hard working Tieck gave much of his work to his daughter Dorothea and to Wolf Heinrich Graf von Baudissin.

Classicism and Romanticism was dominated on the Elbe by painting and literature. However the pendulum of art is always moving. A fantastic person who moved between the styles was responsible for the change to the period of musical flourishment in the 19th century: E. T. A. Hoffmann. Ernst Theodor Amadeus Hoffmann (1776–1822) was poet, composer, conductor, painter and lawyer. A many sided artistic personality, as loved in romanticism. In 1813 Hoffmann takes his job as Kapellmeister in Dresden. You can appreciate his vision of the Dresden Society in his fantastic fairy tale "Der goldne Topf". Hoffmanns mysterious stories are still wonderful lessons. But who still knows his operas "Aurora" and "Undine"? He became one of the founders of the romantic opera through these.

The painting "Überfahrt am Schreckenstein" by Ludwig Richter (1803–1884) is a typical nostalgic picture of the 19th century. Richter taught at the Dresdner Academy.

The Zwinger is the
crowning of the Baroque
on the Elbe. The master
builder of August der
Starke, Matthäus Daniel
Pöppelmann, built it
between 1710 and 1732 as a
festival place for the
Kursächsischer Hof.

The „Freischütz" awoke an unknown enthusiasm. The public had been forced through the magic of romanticism and had cheered the creation of a truly national opera. This was the description a generation later of the effect of Carl Maria von Weber's marvellous creation in the year 1820. The "Freischütz" signalised the triumph of German Romantic Opera. Dresden became one of the main acting locations.

When Carl Maria von Weber arrived in the Elbestadt in 1816 with a respectable contract as Kapellmeister in his pocket this thirty year old had only ten years in front of him for his major works. After the "Freischütz" he composed the opera "Euryanthe" and shortly before his death "Oberon". "Through the woods, through the meadows ..." The aria of Max in the "Freischütz" is something which almost every child in Dresden is able to sing. The "Wolfsschlucht" is a place of attraction outside the gates of the town. It is not only the locals who believe that the Saxon woodland, in which the composer was fond of wondering inspired him to Germany's most popular opera.

Weber was followed in 1842 by Richard Wagner. He was also very young when he took over the position of Hofkapellmeister. He had visited the Kreuzschule in 1827. Wagner rediscovered the opera. A tremendous time started. His operas were musical gun powder, which even today have retained there fire. "Der fliegende Holländer", "Tannhäuser", "Lohengrin" were presented in Dresden.

The opera reformer discovered a friend in Dresden, who became important for the town in a completely different way. The master builder from Altona, Gottfried Semper was brought to the Elb-Florence in 1834. He built the building for the glittering opera period: the Semper Opera House.

Once again, as in the Zwinger, the image of an epoch was depicted in a building. The history of this gigantic urban show piece in vicinity of the Elbe and castle starts in 1841 with its inauguration. The programme included Weber's "Jubelouvertüre" and Goethe's "Torquato Tasso". May 1849: the May-Revolution in Dresden. Semper and Wagner escape and emigrate. Both took part in the uprising. A fire destroyed the Semper Opera House in 1869. A new building is erected in 1878, designed again by Semper and inaugurated with Goethes "Iphigenie". The most outstanding events in the next few decades are the first day and original opening operas of Richard Strauss: "Salome" in 1905, "Electra" in 1909, "Der Rosenkavalier" in 1911 and "Die Frau ohne Schatten" in 1919.

When Dresden is demolished in the bombing night of 13/14th February 1945, so is the opera. The way the blackened ruin is transformed into the glittering Semper Opera House again, is a story of restoration having many tales. The building is reopened exactly forty years later with a production of Carl Maria von Weber's "Freischütz"; the bronzed panther quadriga is pounding into the sky over the portico again. The formal staircase and the foyers display the sumptuous opulence and taste of the 19th century. The show begins long before the curtain is raised, in the auditorium with the 260 candled chandelier, which is also used to balance the acoustics. The curtain itself is however the main attraction. It gives the impression of a well built woman. Surrounded by the allegories of drama and by music. And all around a chain with the pictures of famous artists, including of course Carl Maria von Weber and Richard Wagner.

The delicate dancer on the glass ball of the art academy on the Brühlsche Terrasse is a godess. The courageous Nike crowns a building which occupies the site at the Elbe since 1894 with the pathos signs of eclecticism. Dresden is turned into an industrial town in the second half of the 19th century. The new wealth from flourishing companies producing chemicals, tobacco products, cloth, paper, porcelain and instrument manufacture, is proudly displayed as the *Neureich,* the newly rich so often do. Dresden now has almost 200,000 inhabitants. The Dresdner Bank is founded in 1872. The people of Dresden vote the social democrat August Bebel into the Reichstag. The rich retire to the villa suburbs, which are mainly situated to the east of the town.

At best is the "splendid isolation" on the Weißer Hirsch, the White Stag. Soon one villa after another is rowed along the hilly landscape on the fringe of the Dresden Heide, between Loschwitz and Bühlau. The lucky ones have a view of the Elbe. Those with money recuperate in the sanatorium of Dr. Lahmann. Those who want to, take a trip up the Weißer Hirsch with the mountain railway. A cup of coffee in the "Luisenhof" and you have the whole of Dresden at your feet. Unquestionably, the Weißer Hirsch was one of the finest districts to be found on earth. The bombs have not destroyed it, but the slow deterioration which set in after the war. It was favourable for the scientist Manfred von Ardenne to set up his research laboratories on the Weißer Hirsch after his return from Russia and thus keep some of the houses in a better condition.

Fine buildings are erected after 1850 also in Loschwitz. The vineyards are turned into palace gardens, in which magnificent buildings are built for the factory owner Lingner, the Schloß Albrechtsberg and Schloß Eckberg. A triumvirate of architecture with strongly varying political history. Whoever thinks about the small garden house, in which Friedrich von Schiller once sat and wrote, and at Blasewitz about the Wallenstein-Gustel, also comes onto the bridge which links Loschwitz on the north bank with Blasewitz on the south bank of the Elbe. The people of Dresden experienced their "Blaues Wunder", their blue wonder in 1893. The blue painted suspension bridge is inaugurated. This world wonder of the industrial age has a clear span of 141 metres. A triumph of technology.

In Blasewitz and Loschwitz someone has the idea of counting all the places which end in the letters witz, litz, nitz oder ritz: Rochwitz, Wachwitz, Hosterwitz, Zschachwitz, Tolkewitz, and Pillnitz, Pappritz, Kaditz, Wolfnitz, Nausslitz, Räcknitz, Pestitz, Zschertnitz, Mockritz, Leubnitz, Seidnitz, Dobritz.

A completely different thing is the incomplete list of artists, who were born in Dresden in the second half of the 19th century or around 1900 and became important for the twentieth century: Paula Modersohn-Becker (1876), Erich Kästner (1899), Hermann Glöckner (1889), Hans (1901) and Lea (1906) Grundig. However, a revolution in art began in 1905 in a former shop in the town.

The Elbwiesen, the meadows on the Elbe, form the lovely setting for the famous silhouette of the city, which has been painted, drawn and photographed a thousand times. The highest tower in the sky is the Wettiner Hofkirche out of the 18th century on the right.

Dresden, Berliner Straße 60. In 1905, this was the location of the studio of the painter Erich Heckel. Not a particularly important address. But the former butchers shop was to become the nursing place of a vital rebellion in art. Here the three architectural students Erich Heckel, Ernst Ludwig Kirchner and Karl Schmidt-Rottluff talked their heads off. Down with academic art. Their aim was a sensual, free form, in which colours were to glow a completely unknown fashion. On 7 June 1905 they founded the "Brücke", a group of artists. "From what we had to escape was clear to us. Where we were going to was not so clear", remembered Erich Heckel later. The name "Brücke", bridge, was chosen by the youngest of them, Karl Schmidt-Rottluff, who had just turned the age of 21. Kirchner, Heckel, Schmidt-Rottluff remained the central figures of the group, which soon was joined by Max Pechstein, Otto Müller and, for a short time, Emil Nolde.

These turn of the century young avantgarde in Dresden had their pictures of influence. In the famous Gallery Arnold in the Schloßstraße, they had seen pictures by Vincent van Gogh and Edvard Munch. This wild and anarchic art had given them the creative spurt. The "Brücke" stepped into new areas of art, when they started the redefinition of geometric forms including their graphic interpretation. Their wood cuttings became most well known.

The artists worked a lot together. In summer they moved to the Moritzburger Seen, the lakes, to experience and draw nature. Their life was so closely knit that it is sometimes hard to differentiate between their works in this early period. The acceptance of their rebellion in art was limited. However the rejection was also not so damaging as in the beginning of the Thirties when the narrowed mindedness of the Nazis began to rule. The artists of the "Brücke" were classed as *"entartet"*, decadent and their work was finally banned from museums in 1937. It is hardly a compensation after such a brutal persecution of an artistic movement, that exhibitions after 1945 long queues stood in front of the pictures of these painters.

The artists grouped round Kirchner, Heckel and Schmidt-Rottluff fully understood how to portray their message in these years in Dresden. They enthusiastically mixed in with and influenced the local art scene. A lively exhibition world was created in the town on the Elbe shortly after the turn of the century, as in Berlin, Munich and Cologne. The noble galleries remained at first closed to the painters of the "Brücke" with their flood of colours. Their first exhibition in Dresden took place in a lamp factory. One of the first people to recognise the quality of the new style in painting was Karl Ernst Osthaus. The "Brücke" was allowed to exhibit in his Folkwang-Museum in Hagen/Westphalia even in 1907. Their works were shown in 50 (!) mostly smaller exhibitions up to 1910.

In 1910 the break through came also in Dresden. The Gallery Arnold opened its show rooms to the painters. There was a limited success in terms of recognition and most of all in terms of money. A year later almost every "Brücke" artist had opened a studio in Berlin. However the group quickly disbanded. The external reason was the publication in 1913 of history of the "Brücke" by Ernst Ludwig Kirchner in which he claimed the leadership. There had been trouble years before. The group officially disbanded just a year before the final split in art which resulted from the First World War. The painters had their most creative phase in the years in Dresden and founded German Expressionism together with the Munich group "Blauer Reiter".

„... The examinations are finished for today, but I experienced a jab in the heart with tears of pain in the night again, so that I believe I will be staying here for a few months." This was written by Oskar Kokoschka in 1916 to Herwarth Walden, the publisher of the Berlin Expressionism Magazine "Sturm". The Viennese artist recovered from a serious war wound in Dresden. He actually stayed eight years on the Elbe. He was a highly respected painter. The students of the Kunstakademie treasured him as professor. However Kokoschka never lost status as being an outsider. He will be remembered in the chronicle of the Dresden Boheme through his "Blaue Puppe". Still mourning the loss of his girlfriend Alma Mahler-Werfel, who married the architect Walter Gropius in 1915, Kokoschka built a life size blue doll à la Alma and was not afraid to take this stuffed lady into a box at the Semper Opera. This went on until the "Blaue Puppe" had too much red wine one night at an artists ball and her "life" drained away.

Kokoschka was not a conservative. Different to the many Dresdner, whose hearts still beat for the Kaiser in the Sarrasani Circus on the banks of the Elbe, or for the King of Saxony, who now had to vacate his beautiful Schloß after the proclamation of the Republic in 1918. However after a bullet went through a picture of Rubens in 1920 during a contest between the Left and the Right in the Zwinger, the artist appealed to the public in an open letter that they should preferably fight their disputes in the shooting grounds of the Heide.

Many artists moved to Dresden in the Twenties. It would be quite a euphemism to call this period "golden". The years of hunger after the War followed the economic crisis with the terrible problem of joblessness. The urban image was only slightly changed by new buildings. As in the first decade of the century with Fritz Schumacher, the architect Hans Poelzig was now to become an important teacher of the art of building. However there was hardly money for big projects. The Deutsche Hygiene-Museum, designed by Wilhelm Kreis, was opened in 1930.

On the other hand another form of art flourished. The dancer Mary Wigman had come to Dresden in 1920 and founded her school there. The Wigman style changed ballet as the "Brücke" had been a revolution in painting. The free, dynamic movement of the new school hit the headlines as the "German dance". Harald Kreuzberg taught here the *"Ausdruckstanz"*. Gret Palucca became a pupil of the Wigman-School. She founded her own institute in Dresden in 1925, in which she taught generations of dancers. Her mother in law was Ida Bienert, who collected one of the best avantgarde art collections during the Twenties in Dresden.

Someone who understood how to link the arts came to Dresden in 1919 – the now residential city of the Wettiner: the painter and illustrator Josef Hegenbarth. He had studied at the Kunstakademie and was made professor after the Second World War. His drawings of fairy tales became famous. His archive is still treasured in Dresden.

The tram lines crossed the Postplatz around 1900. Horse carriages are waiting in the middle for passengers.

In 1720 Matthäus Daniel Pöppelmann began with the building of the water and hill palace of Schloß Pillnitz. It today houses the Museum für Kunsthandwerk.

In the Twenties, both Lea and Hans Grundig, born in Dresden, were involved in art against war and fascism. Both escaped the persecution of the Nazis – Lea emigrated, Hans was arrested and was put in a concentration camp – and both were made professors in 1945 in Dresden. The sharpest, dogged social critic amongst the artists was Otto Dix after the First World War. His experiences of war, in which he had been wounded several times, developed into a trauma for him. He unscrupulously drew and painted his fellow society. He had studied in Dresden before the war. In 1919 he founded the "Dresdner Sezession". Eight years later he was made a professor of the Kunstakademie. Today his most gigantic and horrific painting "Der Krieg" is kept in the Staatliche Kunstsammlung. The triptych – a painting of the century – finished in 1932 is both a memorial and premonition. The warning anticipation against war could only be shown for a short time. Otto Dix was the first to be thrown from his post in 1933 by the Nazis.

In the same year the new rulers of the town also defame some of Dix's paintings in the exhibition "Spiegelbilder des Verfalls".

Dresden ist turned into a "brown" city in the same unbelievable speed as in the rest of Germany. The conductor Fritz Busch is pulled from his rostrum in the Semper Opera by rowdy Nazis. The beginning of the end. The fall of Dresden twelve years later is an inferno, whose shadow still casts over the town today.

This photograph of a lane in the Altstadt is from 1932. On the left you can buy home made sausage goods and on the right "clean guest rooms" are on offer.

The perfection of the
square in front of the
magnificence of the
Zwinger, with its beautiful
buildings, from which the
Wallpavillon at the north
side is perhaps the best.
Behind the arch is a staircase leading to the Wall-
anlagen.

The bathing pool of the nymphs at the Zwinger shows the completed harmony between architecture and sculpture. Pöppelmanns design blends with the sculptural ornamentation of Balthasar Permoser into an exciting total artistic composition.

The detail of figure work of the sculptures of Balthasar Permoser is of the highest quality. The stone was brought by the sculptor from the nearby Elbsand-steingebirge.

The Goldene Reiter, the sculptural riding figure of August der Starke created in 1732 is the symbol of the Neustädter Markt (designed by Jean Joseph Vinache, cooper work by Ludwig Wiedemann).

The restored Stallhof at the Schloß served as background for knights tournaments at the time of Count Moritz (1521–1553). The Renaissance complex is overshadowed by the tower of the Hofkirche built some 200 years later.

DU ALTER STAMM,
SEI STETS ERNEUT
IN EDLER FÜRSTEN
REIHE,
WIE ALLE ZEIT
DEIN VOLK DIR
WEIHT
DIE ALTE DEUTSCHE
TREUE.

The portion from the Prince's Procession on the outer wall of the Stallhof demonstrates the respect with which the House of Wettin was honoured in the 19th century. The illustration by Wilhelm Walther which was created from 1872 to 1876 was manufactured in weather proof tiles from Meißen in 1907.

The detail picture of the Stallhof shows the intricacy of the elevational ornament. The Renaissance bulding was destroyed in 1945, as the whole of the historic city centre of Dresden. Amazing attention to detail has been put into the restoration work.

The Hofkirche, which was built by the son of August der Starke, Friedrich August (1696–1763) from the Italian architect Gaetano Chiaveri, is deco-rated again with the restored Silbermann organ. It is the biggest creation of Johann Gottfried Silbermann (1683–1753).

The Semperoper glows in restored beauty since 1985. Gottfried Sempers major creation (1871–1878) is crowned by the bronzed panther quadriga of the sculptor Johannes Schilling.

The vestibule of the Semperoper displays again the festive magnificence as so loved in the 19th century. The craftsmen created a true wonder in their restoration. They created wooden columns to look as though they were made out of marble.

You need a pair of opera glasses to truly appreciate the small scale detail. It is visual treat right up into the furthest corner.

A monarch no longer sits in the kings box of the Semperoper. Anyone can sit in the upper circle and pretend to act out the role of royalty.

The Straße der Befreiung, created by August der Starke as his main street in the Neustadt, is again a Boulevard for sauntering. The former flat of the Kügelgen family can be found at No. 13 in the row of restored old buildings, which is today the Museum für die Dresdner Früh-romantik.

The Prager Straße is symbolic of new Dresden, which began in 1945. The concrete buildings stand apart from the historic buildings.

The Trümmerfrau was the first monument erected after the destruction of the city. The sculpture which was made at the beginning of the Fifties remembers the brave women of Dresden.

View of a street in the Neustadt. Not only the cobble
stones are old, but also the
car (left): a IFA F 8, built
1953.

The suspension railway
leads from Loschwitz to
Oberloschwitz. One of the
most beautiful views is
offered from here.

The angel on the roof of the   clearly shows the scars
Rathaus looks at the new   made by the war.
Dresden. The view in 1945
from here was on a desert
of ruins. The rebuilding

Martin Luther in front of the ruins of the Frauenkirche. Dresdens oldest church collapsed in on itself on 15 February 1945 after the Fire of Dresden. A monument against war.

"No more war!", Käthe Kollwitz' oriflamme again war has become a warning for this century. The famous designer, who used her art to protest against the suffering of people, died in Moritzburg near Dresden on 22 April 1945. In no less than ten weeks before war had carried out a so terrible act only a few kilometres away from Moritzburg, so that today any kind of description results in an incredible horror. The fall of Dresden happened at a time when the fate of the war had already been decided. During the night of the 13th to 14th February British and American bombers raided the city and killed thousands of people. Industrial areas and traffic junctions were not attacked. The inner city was the direct target with its buildings from seven centuries and the surrounding residential districts. There were more than a hundred thousand killed in just one night, after which no day followed. The sky was black over the city, which had been turned into a graveyard. When the Red Army marched into Dresden on 8. May, it was in total ruins.

Dresden 1945. The angel cut from stones looks from the roof of the Rathaus over the fallen city.

The view travels far into
the river landscape from the
Bastei in the Elbsandsteingebirge. The hills supplied
the stones for the Baroque
monumental buildings of
Dresden.

If you do not want to walk, you can ride. The cable railway leads up the Weißer Hirsch.

At the foot of the hill is Pillnitz. Its park and palace complex is one of the nicest attractions around Dresden.

Not only the landscape is mild on the Elbe; so is the climate. Vines grow in sheltered positions as here in Coswig not far from Dresden.

The old Elb-town Meißen is worth viewing for at least four reasons: the beautiful situation, the number of historic buildings, its good wine and of course the porcelain factory.

The pheasantry is a jewel in the spacious complex of Schloß Moritzburg. The building with its square plan was built in 1769—1782 by Johann Daniel Schade

Jagdschloß Moritzburg is situated like a fairy palace in the middle of a picturesque lakeland in front of the gates of Dresden. The complex was started under the direction of Count Moritz in the 16th century. Its strongest quality was given to it in the Baroque period of August der Starke in the 18th century. Today the castle is a museum to the Baroque in its highest magnificence.

The wine which comes from
the slopes of the Elbe is
still a tip for connoisseurs.
This vineyard district has
however a long tradition
and the manors of the
vineyards shave a culture
stretching far back.

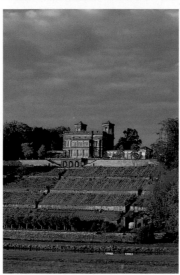

The lovely hill of Dresden, Weißer Hirsch, was occupied by villas and smaller palaces in the second half of the 19th century. The clients were fond of imitating the styles of former periods.

The nicest view of the town is from the hilly right bank of the river where villas and vineyards are evidence of former prosperity.

The silhouette of Dresden in a dramatic evening light. The winged goddess of victory, Nike, hovers on the glass dome of the Kunst-hochschule at the Brühlsche Terrasse to the left. The tower of the Hofkirche points into the sky on the right.

The beauty of present day rebuilt Dresden is flavoured by melancholy. The buildings built after the war stand uncompromisingly adjacent to old and restored magnificence, or buildings which are still in ruins.

"Nu" is a word which is used by true people of Dresden to begin or end every second sentence. "Nu" means yes. Behind this is hidden a friendly, lively mentality, which is also fashioned by the phrase, "Mein Gudster, meine Gudste", meaning something like "my dearest". A mentality which helps to survive. The first cultural signs of survival were surprisingly seen in this city of ruins. Theatre opened again in Dresden only five months after the destruction. Lessings "Nathan der Weise". The main actor was Erich Ponto. Joseph Keilbarth conducted a performance of "Figaros Hochzeit" in August 1945. Keilbarth became musical director, Ponto musical manager. The Kreuzchor performed again under the direction of Rudolf Mauersberger.

Thus perhaps, the overpowering communist government in Dresden in the following period was better to accept than in other places. It was easy to drift off into a dream in the Gemäldegalerie Alte Meister, in front of the "Sixtinian Madonna" or the prospects of Canaletto, in the sparkle of the treasures of the Grünes Gewölbe, away from the everday dreariness.

The prescribed social realism was undermined by a sub-culture of personal fantasy. When the "Patriarch of the Dresden Modern Movement", Hermann Glöckner was not quite in favour with the SED, the ruling political party in der GDR, with his abstract paintings, a celebration of a quite special character was organised for his 85th birthday in 1974. Works from Glöckner were hung in eight different private flats, showing the separate phases of his work. The exhibition stretched from Radebeul to Wachwitz.

Formerly large art exhibitions of the art of the GDR were held every five years. The replacement of social realism through a new freedom in art was documented here much earlier than was realised in the West.

The champion of art rides for Dresden since 1956. August der Starke and his stallion at the beginning of the Straße der Befreiung stand there so fantastic in glittering gold as if they have fallen out of a dream of an undestroyed glowing Dresden.

This irradiating, powerful triumphant rider is the symbolic figure of a resurrected Dresden. The path stretches out from here over the Augustusbrücke to Baroque Dresden or through the lanes of the Neustadt to Loschwitz, Pillnitz and up the hills, which follow the river to become dramatic canyons in the Elbsandsteingebirge.

Dresden with its museums, its opera, its theatre has become a city of culture again. Lively also through the many artists who work in the Elbe-town. The past is stronger linked to the future as in any other city. This can also be seen in the newly erected island of luxury; the expensive hotels Bellevue and Dresdner Hof. Both new buildings integrate existing older buildings. A Baroque Bürgerhaus at Bellevue and a restored "Sekundogenitur" (called after the seond Prince) at the Dresdner Hof as fine as the restaurant situated on the Brühlsche Terrasse. That too: You can live well again in Dresden.

The **Albertinum** at the Brühlschen Garten (formerly the Arsenal, rebuilt 1887) contains today the **Galerie Neue Meister** with important painting from the period of Romanticism, Impressionism, Expressionism, Cubism and the present day art. The treasures from the **Grünes Gewölbe** can be found under the same roof until the restoration work on the Schloß have been completed. This unique collection of precious artifacts, founded by August der Starke, reached a climax in the work of the goldsmith Johann Melchior Dinglinger, with the architect Pöppelmann and the sculptor Permoser who formed that creative triumvirate of art at the court of August der Starke. Also in the Albertinum: **Antikensammlung** and **Münzkabinett** (Antique collection and coin collection).

The **Augustusbrücke** links the Altstadt with the Neustadt, which in reality is also an old town. It was designed by the master builder of August der Starke, Matthäus Daniel Pöppelmann in 1717 and through its arches was to reflect the image of the Rialto Bridge in Venice.

The luxury hotels Bellevue and Dresdner Hof have historic buildings integrated into them. The new building of the Bellevue on the north bank of the Elbe is merged into a Baroque Bürgerhaus. The new building of the Dresdner Hof at the Neumarkt is integrated into the **Sekundogenitur** at the Brühlsche Terrasse. The Sekundogenitur, named after the second prince, is a neo-Baroque building from 1897 and was an exhibition hall before the war.

Das Blaue Wunder, the bridge between Loschwitz and Blasewitz was opened in 1893. The then avantgarde steel construction is painted blue.

The Brühlsche Terrasse (Brühl Garden) on the south bank of the Elbe (landing stage of the Weiße Flotte) was linked in 1814 for the public by a spacious staircase to the Theaterplatz (the **Museum für Mineralogie und Geologie** adjacent). The beautiful walkway, famous for its marvellous view "balcony of Europe" got its name from the Prime Minister of Friedrich August, Count Brühl (1700–1763), (see also page 6).

The Deutsche Hygiene-Museum on the western edge of the Großer Garten, built to the plans of the architect Wilhelm Kreis was opened in 1930. Main attraction: the glass human. The museum was started through the idea of the industrialist Karl August Lingner (1861–1916), who built up a large pharmacy industry in Dresden during the Gründerzeit.

The Dreikönigskirche dominates the winding lanes of the Neustadt. The Gothic building from 1404 was several times destroyed or rebuilt. In 1731 the church had to be moved and be rebuilt on another site because of the town planning of August der Starke. It was in the way of his main street (Straße der Befreiung). The 87 metre high tower is the symbol of the Neustadt. The church has been rebuilt in stages after it was completely burned out in 1945.

The Elbcastles Schloß Albrechtsberg, the Lingner-Schloß and Schloß Eckberg are reached from the Bautzner Straße. They were built in the second half of the nineteenth century in the vineyards of Loschwitz. Schloß Eckberg has become an hotel again. Schloß Albrechtsberg was made into a pinoneer palace under the socialist regime, the Lingner-Schloß was made into a centre for communication and education, seat of the Dresden "Club of Intelligence".

The Frauenkirche, the oldest church of Dresden, whose dome was world famous, is still a ruin today, a monument against war (see also page 5).

The Gemäldegalerie Alte Meister ist to be found in the building with which the architect Gottfried Semper closed the open side of the Zwinger in 1854. All the great names of the period can be found together in the Dresden collection of European master painters from the period 15th to 18th centuries: Dürer, van Dyck, El Greco, Holbein, Leonardo da Vinci, Rembrandt, Rubens, Tintoretto, Titian, Velasquez, Vermeer van Delft. The main attractions of the collection are the "Sixtinian Madonna" by Raffael and the town prospects by Canaletto. The main part of the collection of the Galerie Alte Meister was put together by the son of August der Starke, Friedrich August in the 18th century.

The Goldene Reiter, the riding figure of August der Starke on the Neustädter Markt was produced in cooper in a two year work by Ludwig Wiedemann (1732–34). The monument was given an oil gold leafing in 1956.

The Großer Garten, is situated to the east of the Altmarkt. It was formed as a Baroque garden in the 18th century and is today as Dresdens largest park a recreational area with sport facilities. The Starcke-Palace from the 17th century, formerly the oldest Baroque building of Dresden has been partially restored after the destruction in 1945.

The Hochschule für bildende Künste, near the Albertinum at the Brühlsche Terrasse was built by Konstantin Lipsius (1885–1894). Oskar Kokoschka and Otto Dix, amongst others, taught there at the beginning of the twentieth century.

The Hofkirche at the Residenzschloß was designed in 1738 by the Italian architect Gaetano Chiaveri. Today the restored building with sculptures by Permoser is used again as a catholic church. The Silbermann organ is the only work existing from the famous organ builder of the 18th century, which could be preserved in Dresden. The Royal Tombs of princes of the House of Wettin are in the crypt of the Hofkirche including a capsule containing the heart of August der Starke.

The Jägerhof, east of the Augustusbrücke has one of the oldest parts of the town with its west wing from 1617. Today it houses the **Museum für Volkskunst.**

The Japanese Palace, west of the Augustusbrücke was erected at the beginning of the 18th century as Gesandtschaftsgebäude, an ambassadors building. The palace later became a porcelain museum and library. After the destruction in 1945 parts of the local history collection of Dresden is now housed in restored rooms.

The Johanneum, which can be found at the Neumarkt has also had a very mixed history. Built in Renaissance style in the 16th century, it first served as stable for horses. After several extensions it finally housed the art collection of the princes in the 18th century. The Johanneum with its splendid open staircase is the only building of the Neumarkt to be restored after 1945. The Neumarkt was completely destroyed as can still be seen in the ruins of the Frauenkirche. Today the Johanneum serves as **Verkehrsmuseum** (Transport-Museum).

The Kreuzkirche at the Altmarkt can be traced back to the beginning of the 13th century. It was often destroyed across the centuries. Famous musicians have been produced from the associated Kreuzchor (Richard Wagner, Peter Schreier). The choir holds regular concerts in the church.

The Kupferstichkabinett (engravings chamber), in the Güntzstraße possesses one of the best drawing collections of the world. The first sheets were purchased by the elector August in the 16th century for his art chamber. The collection stretches from the German and Italian Renaissance up to the present day and covers some 20,000 sheets.

The Landhaus houses the Town History Museum since 1965. As the only historic building in the Thälmann-Straße it was erected in the 18th century and was restored after almost total destruction in 1945.

The Residenzschloß between Theaterplatz and Brühlsche Terrasse, damaged in 1945 is presently being restored since 1984. The beginnings of this building complex go back to the time of Moritz Count of Saxony (1521–1553). The restored **Stallhof** is already an attraction. This Renaissance building was formerly for duelling tournaments. A sgrafitto more than one hundred metres long is on the outer wall, the Augustusstraße: the **Fürstenzug,** the Princes Procession, a historical depiction of the House of Wettin, designed 1872 and glazed in 25,000 tiles from Meißen in 1907.

The Semperoper is situated at Theaterplatz, which is at the other end of the Sempergalerie linked to the Zwinger. The opera house, inaugurated in 1878 and designed by Gottfried Semper is the focus of this famous square of the 19th century. The Semperoper, destroyed in 1945, has been completely restored to full magnificence being reopened in 1985 with a production of Carl Maria von Weber's "Freischütz". The panther quadriga of Ariadne and the Dionysus over the opera portico and the rider statue of King Johann at the Theaterplatz were created by the sculptor Johannes Schilling (1828–1910), from whose workshop the statue of Gottfried Semper also comes, which stands at the Brühlsche Terrasse (see also page 16).

The Straße der Befreiung begins at the Neustädter Markt. Several historic houses were rebuilt on the left hand side of the pedestrian zone. This includes the **Kügelgenhaus,** in which is housed the **Museum für die Dresdner Frühromantik.**

The Weißer Hirsch (White Stag) can be reached either from Loschwitz via the Bautzner Straße or with the cable railway. The former select villa district was previously a Kurort. There is a magnificent view of Dresden from the restaurant **Luisenhof** (see also page 17).

The Zwinger counts as one of the most beautiful buildings of European Baroque. The whole square complex completed 1710–1732 under the appointment of August der Starke for court festivities is the marvellous creation of the architect Daniel Pöppelmann. The sculptures were created by the sculptor Balthasar Permoser. The festive architecture is crowned by three pavilions. The square which was world famous for its gay and frivolous nature crowned the Dresden Baroque and the Augustinian Age. The restoration work on the buildings destroyed in 1945 was completed in 1964. The attractions in the Zwinger are the Gemäldegalerie Alte Meister and the Porzellanmuseum (see also page 8).

Places of interest in the surrounding district

The Erzgebirge south of Dresden was important to Saxony for centuries because of the existence of large quantities of raw minerals. The nicest area to visit is the Müglitztal with its marvellous castles and fortifications (Weesenstein, Bärenstein, Lauenstein and Dohna). There is a mine to be visited at Altenberg. An exhibition of the organ maker Johann Gottfried Silbermann, who was born there in 1683, can be seen in the Renaissanceschloß of Frauenstein.

The Baroque Garden of Großsedlitz, situated 15 kilometres south east of Dresden, was considered to be the most beautiful of its age in Saxony. The Baroque staircase "Stille Musik" designed by Matthäus Daniel Pöppelmann is of special harmony. The palace building was opened in 1874. There is nothing remaining of the garden which belonged to the Baroque palace from the time of August der Starke.

The Town of Meißen, 25 kilometres away from Dresden down the River Elbe, which can also be reached by boat, is famous for its beautiful location, its historic townscape, its porcelain and its wine. The inner town is under conservation. The House of Wettin chose Meißen as its residency in the 12th century. The Albrechtsburg and the Dom were built in the Gothic period. Construction of the Domherrenhöfe and the Kornhaus began after 1400. The late-Gothic Rathaus and the Frauenkirche with its porcelain chimes are worth seeing. The porcelain factory (with exhibition) founded in 1710 can be visited by the public.

The Jagdschloß Moritzburg, ten kilometres north west of Dresden situated in a nature reserve with many lakes remains in its Baroque splendour. August der Starke appointed three architects to build a palace out of the hunting palace of Count Moritz: Matthäus Daniel Pöppelmann, Zacharias Longuelune, Johann Christoph Knöffel. The magnificent Baroque building with its precious interior was built 1723–1736. The impressive Allee der Balustradenstatuen, on which the sculptor Balthasar Permoser was also occupied, is also famous. There is an exhibition of artistic craftswork in the **Barockmuseum** of the Moritzburg.

Schloß Pillnitz, to the south east of Dresden can be best reached using a boat of the Weiße Flotte. The water and mountain palace was built in 1724 by Matthäus Daniel Pöppelmann, just as the the small Weinbergkirche to the north. The architect Christian Friedrich Schuricht reformed the park and palace complex through the buildings of the new palace and the Chinese pavilion. The Schloßpark is famous because of its variety of gardens and rare plants (Dutch Garden, conifer woods, chestnut alleys, nine metre high Japanese Camellia).

In Radebeul, to the north western edge of Dresden, are three small palaces which can be visited: Wackerbarths Palais, which was the retirement place of the ministers of August der Starke built by architect Johann Christoph Knöffel; Schloß Hoflößnitz from the 17th century, which today has a museum on the history of the local wine making, and the Bennoschlößchen, the manor house of a vineyard which was constructed at the beginning of the 17th century. Radebeul is also the town of Karl May. The **Karl-May-Museum** has information on the writer and has a collection of religious and daily life articles of red indians.

The Sächsische Schweiz (Elbsandsteingebirge) is an unusually attractive area to the south east of Dresden. It can be reached by boat (to Bad Schandau). The Tafelbergland is crossed by deep canyons. The mountains are a famous climbing area through their vertical rock cliffs. There are many marvellous view points with wide panoramas of the Elbe landscape. Most famous is the **Bastei.** Other places to visit are the **Festung Königstein** with the Georgenburg, the Kurort Rathen with its stage of stone as well as Bad Schandau with the interesting church St. Johannis.